T0142525

50 + 1

The 50 Most Egregious Errors found on the Internet
And, of course, There is always One more

+
Series
Reading
Writing
Thinking
Listening
Personal Safety
Jury Nullification
The Appendices
A – Words: Acronyms & Initialism
B – Quotations & Ponderables

NATE TANGUAY

50 + 1

iUniverse books may be ordered through booksellers or by contacting:

iUniverse
1663 Liberty Drive
Bloomington, IN 47403
www.iuniverse.com
1-800-Authors (1-800-288-4677)

ISBN: 978-1-5320-8590-1 (sc)
ISBN: 978-1-5320-8591-8 (e)

Print information available on the last page.

iUniverse rev. date: 11/23/2019

Table of Contents

Dedication

This book is dedicated to my online friends.
You know who you are.
And to those who have learned from me,
Even though they did not always realize it.

Introduction

Although some of the information in the book may seem simplistic—it is not.

In Chapter One, 50+1, are the most improper word usages on the internet. As I have obtained each of these egregious errors from there, it stands to reason that this chapter will help writers to be more grammatically correct. As English, to many, is not their primary language, this chapter should become their go-to resource.

Punctuation tells the reader exactly what the author meant. Chapter Two covers the 17 primary marks out of 24. Why not the other seven? Those seven are almost never used and most are not on the QWERTY keyboard.

Read for a reason, to understand what the author is trying to convey. Chapter Three, "Be A Perspicacious Reader," will help to not only understand the words, but also the inflection of the author. Read about what is important to you.

Writers are readers. To improve your writing you have to become a reader. Chapter Four, "Improving Your Writing," will help you along that path.

What about thinking? Chapter Five, "Thinking," will show how the thought process works. Ideas come to us like water in a gentle stream . . . not like in a tsunami. Many people don't think before they speak, write, or act. That is why they get in trouble or sound unschooled.

What more peaceful endeavor can one have than to listen to silence. My 10-part Series on listening that I posted on Facebook a few years ago is incorporated in Chapter Six, "Listening."

Chapter Seven, "Personal Safety," I wrote this for a lecture for bank employees at the request of the branch manager. Think of your own situation and think of other ways to keep yourself and your loved ones safer.

What is this most powerful tool that we freemen have to preserve our freedoms. Chapter Eight, "Jury Nullification," will tell you how.

Appendix A, "Words." Some of my favorites.

Appendix B, "Quotations, Ponderables, and Phases of Surrender," will most probably give you an insight on how I think and who I am.

My Websites and Pages

Pledge to never register or surrender your weapons of self defense.
www.secondamendmentwarrior.com

Driving and Personal Safety Tips.
www.youarestupidif.com

Patriots Against Gun Confiscation
www.facebook.com/GunConfiscation

Firearms & Survival Articles
www.facebook.com/GunArticles

Jury Nullification
www.facebook.com/Jury-Nullification-167859696652904

I Killed My Child
www.facebook.com/childrentrafficdeaths

Gun Confiscation
www.facebook.com/citizens

Grammar Lessons
www.facebook.com/csinate/?modal=admin_todo_tour

OTHER BOOKS BY
THE AUTHOR

Penal Code Handbook
For Connecticut Police Officers

Dispatcher's Guide
To Crimes/Incidents in Progress

Police Officer's Response Guide
To Crimes/Incidents in Progress

ARTICLES

Beretta Take-Down
One Size Fits All

ONE

50 + 1

The Most Common Errors Found on The Internet

What is a word?
A sound or combination of sounds
That has a meaning
And is spoken or written.
—Webster's Dictionary

"That has a meaning," so it should be chosen wisely.

One must not realize just how ignorant one appears,
When making an egregious error.

The Glaring Error

(Improper Word Usage)

The Glaring Error is the phrase used … to signify an error that marks one as unobservant or uneducated, or even stupid or as having some other egregious failing. It simply identifies a mistake that is immediately apparent to the perpetrator's reader or listener, and the reader or listener, recognizing the error, jumps to the conclusion that the writer or speaker is a dunce. – "Writing Clear Paragraphs," Robert B. Donald, James D. Moore, Betty Richmond Morrow, Lillian Griffith Wargetz, Kathleen Werner. — Sixth Edition.

Some examples of glaring errors; if the wrong word is used.

The number indicates the order in which I observed the glaring error.

a, an (25)

Whether to use A or AN depends on whether the next word starts with a vowel or sounds like a vowel. "old" starts with o, a vowel therefore AN old priest would be correct.

Ex.: A hour would be incorrect even though the word hour starts with a consonant, because hour sounds like our, a vowel sound; therefore, AN hour would be correct.

A person would be correct as P is and person sounds like a consonant so A is correct.

It all depends on the sound of the following word.

If it sounds like a vowel then use AN. If it sounds like a consonant then use A.

Using a or an before a U word. Ex.: a unicorn; an umbrella.

aloud, allowed (27)

aloud = louder than your normal conversational voice. To holler or scream.

allowed = given permission to do something or to take part in an activity.

You're allowed to talk aloud during recess.

attacked, attached (26)

"We are being invaded by a foreign culture attacked to foreign laws."

attacked = To set upon with violent force.

Attached = connected or joined to something.

break, brake (6)

break = taking time out or cutting someone some slack.

brake = things on the car that helps to slow it down.

buy, by (19)

buy = To go to a store and get something that you pay for.

I like to BUY my clothes when they're on sale.

by = close to : near - Let's go BY the ocean so we can see the boats.

So as to go along - Let's go BY a different route.

Or through - If the door is locked we can enter BY the window. He went right BY them without being seen.

At, during - He studied by night. Be home by 2 pm.

cite, site, sight (32)

cite = to say or write what an author said, or quote from a book.

Quote from an authoritative source; generally to try to prove your point or to convince another.

in law: cited, commanded to appear in a court of law.

Lawyers usually cite prior cases to convince the judge to vote in their favor.

site = a place, a location.

He asked the building inspector, "Can I build on this site?" (land).

The construction boss told him to go to the site. The place where they're building something.

sight = has to do with your eyes. A blind person has no sight.

If you can see me then, obviously, you have sight.

concur, conquer (37)

"The overall teachings of ISLAM is to concur the world by any means, . . ."

concur = agree with

conquer = take over by force

conservation, conversation (38)

"As if that idea is not already sufficiently nauseating, the conservation occurred over lunch."

conservation = to protect something

conversation = two people talking to each other

disgust, discuss (31)

disgust = feeling of revulsion or profound disapproval aroused by something offensive.

discuss = talking about a subject

Let's discuss this during our next conversation.

due, do, dew (12)

due = the time that something, such as a bill or report, must be paid or completed

do = performance, involved in an activity

dew = moisture on the grass in the morning caused by the cooling of the air.

excepted, accepted (28)

excepted = to leave out.

accepted = to be included. He was accepted into the fraternity.

fare, fair (50)

fare = the money a passenger on public transportation has to pay.

fair = in accordance with the rules or standards.

Also with complexion and hair – a blonde person.

fine, find (33)

"YES PHILLIP YOUR RIGHT. RUBIO AND CRUZ THESE NEED TO GO FINE A WOMEN. AND THEY NEED TO FINE SOMETHING TO DO BUT THEY NEED TO GET OUT OF THE PRESIDENT RUNNING," (Paraphrased).

fine = good, acceptable.

find = locate. I lost my keys. Will you help me FIND them?

I'm going to FIND a FINE woman to go out with.

Consistency here is the key. She broke every grammar rule in the book. Why is one in such a hurry to prove to one's readers that they are a dunce? Posting in caps is rude and hard to read. One should never write when angry.

hay, hey (21)

hay = the stuff that cows eat. Hay, look out! the cow is trying to eat you.

hey = used as an exclamation (!) to call attention; hey, look out!

to express pleasure, surprise; hey! what's going on

informal hello: used as a greeting; hey there.

hell, he'll (20)

This error is not directly related to this series but as I've seen it too often, it's a way to jump into punctuation.

hell = the nether realm of the devil and the demons in which the damned suffer everlasting punishment —

Bad people go to hell when they die instead of Heaven.

often used in curses. <go to hell>

or as a generalized term of abuse <the hell with it>

exclamations: <war is hell> <I had one hell (lousy) of a day>

(There are no apostrophes in hell.)

he'll = Contraction of two words, HE WILL. (Sounds like heel, the part of a shoe).

He'll go home when he feels like it. HE WILL go home …

He said, "whatever happens 'he'll always love her'". …HE WILL always …

If you said, "hell always love her," wouldn't make any sense.

(Although the words don't sound the same a few people enunciate them the same; therefore, to them, it makes no difference whether they use an apostrophe in hell.)

(Anyone who uses an apostrophe in hell will probably end up there).

here, hear (10)

here = a specific place.

hear = when talk or noise enters the ear.

If you don't have EAR you don't have HEAR.

Come HERE so I can HEAR you better.

insight, incite (40)

"use of physical force under the circumstances would further insight the crowd and produce more violent behavior."

Comment from a police department regarding rioters assaulting Trump supporters.

insight = 1. an instance of apprehending the true nature of a thing, especially through intuitive understanding: an insight into 18th-century life.

2. penetrating mental vision or discernment; faculty of seeing into inner character or underlying truth.

incite = to stir, encourage, or urge on; stimulate or prompt to action;

to incite a crowd to riot. (Webster's dictionary).

it's, its (3)

it's = contraction of it is, or it has.

it's time . . . . It is time to sleep.

it's been a long time . . .It has been a long time.

its = possessive.

Charity is its own reward. Its mother died, so the calf had to be fed by a human.

When in doubt, use "it is." If it doesn't make sense then use its: no apostrophe.

knew, new. (9)

knew = past tense of know;

Something I've known for awhile. Information stored in the brain.

new = never used before.

I like NEW clothes, not used clothes.

Don't say, not old clothes. Even though something may be old, it may never have been used; therefore, it's still new.

know, no. (8)

know = things of the mind, present knowledge. I know that.

no = negative exclamation, opposite of yes, doesn't agree.

loose, lose (11)

loose = not tight.

lose = opposite of win; misplace an object, you lose it.

manors, manners (14)

manors = big houses.

manners = social etiquette.

His mother told him to watch his manners at the party.

pole, poll, pool (29)

"another pole they ain't talking about . . ." Why aren't they talking about that stick?

poll = survey of how people think about a particular subject.

pole = a round stick. A flag pole.

Geographical pole = points that a planet rotates on, the North/South poles.

pole = as in a pole position that a horse may start from in a race.

pool = a small, deep body of water.

A swimming pool or a quiet place in a river. "Still waters run deep" — so be careful.

polish, Polish. (15)

polish = what you put on your shoes or polish the table

Polish = the nationality of the people who live in Poland.

The capital P refers to people; the small p refers to an inanimate item or compound.

It's also not pronounced the same.

quits, quiet (49)

quits = stops performing. Gives up.

quiet = no noise. Be quiet, I'm trying to study.

rains, reigns (48)

rains = verb. 3rd person present. It rains every time I want to go golfing.

reigns = to rule. To hold royal office. King and queen.

road, rode (24)

"when she road a mans coat tails all the way"

road = is the area that you drive your car on.

rode = past participle of ride. I rode my bike on the road. "she rode a man's coat."

seem, seam (44)

". . . and families are being ripped apart at the seems."

seems = to appear to be, feel, do, etc.:

She seems better this morning.

seams = the lines formed by sewing together pieces of cloth.

It would have been a great metaphor if the proper word had been used.

seen, scene (34)

seen = something you saw; have you seen the movie yet?

scene = a view of a mountain would make a wonderful scene;

You can make a scene by acting out loudly in an obnoxious way.

soul v. sole (22)

"Obama's immigration plan is costing American lives for the soul purpose of getting votes for the democrats."

soul = the spiritual part of a person that is believed to give life to the body and in many religions is believed to live forever

sole = belonging exclusively or otherwise limited to one usually specified individual, unit, or group — Synonyms: exclusive, single.

steal, still (41)

"I have one on my front porch and I steal use it." (I hope he meant it to be funny).

steal = take (another person's property) without permission or legal right and without intending to return it.

still = up to and including the present or the time mentioned; even now (or then) as formerly.

succeeded, seceded (43)

"I thought CA...subsided, succeeded or something like that."

Referring to whether California was thinking about seceding.

succeeded = to accomplish a goal in your favor.

seceded = to withdraw from a country, group or association.

tails, tales (45)

". . . dead men tell no tails."

Response to the story about the lawyer who committed suicide by crashing his car and shooting himself in the back of the head three times.

"The good news is now most people who read know that all major events covered by the MSM are Hoaxes and false flags pushing an agenda and dead men tell no tails."

tails = the hindmost part of an animal. My dog has a tail and so does a cow.

tales = a narrative that relates the details of some real or imaginary event, incident, or case; story:

I tell the tale about my dog's tail. It is an extension of his spine and you can pull him out of a hole by his tail without hurting him. It's a

West Highland White Westie. This is a true tale. This one made my day. ROFL. I can't stop laughing.

they're, there, their (2)

they're = contraction of they are;

there = a place or state of mind;

their = possessive, belongs to them.

They're (they are) going there (the place) to get their things, (the things belong to them).

through, threw (39)

A comment about the book, *A Little Life*.

"val read it and through it away...."

through = passing from one place to another by an enclosed edifice

A tunnel is an edifice. The train went THROUGH the tunnel.

threw = to discard

thru = is acceptable in place of through in informal writing, in texting, and in certain

disciplines as long as everyone in that discipline agrees.

Val didn't like the book so she discarded it in the trash . . . She threw it away.

then, than (16)

then = "A Wrinkle In Time." Not really, but it does have to do with time. Sequence of events.

We will do this THEN that. This is first and later we will do that.

Let's have dinner then go to the movie.

than = comparison between people, things or a combination of, such as in a simile.

I am smarter THAN you. The sun is hotter THAN the Earth.

to, too, two (4)

to = used to indicate the place, person, or thing that someone or

something moves towards.

I'm going to work.

too = a lot, too much. You're too stupid.

two = the number two, between the 1 and the 3. I bought two (2) tomatoes.

trader, traitor (36)

"By by you TRADER"

(Re. George Will abandoning the GOP party because of Trump).

trader = a person who buys, sells, or exchanges goods.

traitor = a person who is not loyal to his or her own country, friends, etc. :

a person who betrays a country or group of people by helping or supporting an enemy.

try, trys, tries (23) (Person used TRYS for TRIES)

try = attempt to do something. I'm going to TRY sky diving.

trys = the name of a "touchdown" in Rugby. He scored three trys.

tries = plural of try. He tries to be good; but, . . . After several tries he was successful.

tried = past tense. He tried, but failed to make the team.

trying = present tense. He's trying on his new clothes.

waist, waste (13)

waist = the middle part of your body. Put your belt around your waist

waste = garbage, unusable leftovers

(My brain froze for 5 minutes on this one).

ware, wear (and maybe where). (17)

ware = articles (as pottery or dishes) of fired clay <earthenware>;

short for aware.

I like your new dishware.

wear = to use or have (something) as clothing : to have (a shirt, pants, etc.) over part of your body.

You look so handsome when you WEAR a tuxedo. Are you going to WEAR that old dress again?

week, weak (42)

". . . the government could not justify it motion to lift the stay. It's rebuttal was week."

week = has 7 days, 4 each month, 52 in a year.

weak = puny, not strong, gets beat up a lot.

we'll, well (50+1)

we'll = contraction of we will. We will be there.

well = in a good or satisfactory way. Also refers to being healthy. I'm feeling well now.

also a well = a hole in the ground that contains water.

we're, where (47)

we're = contraction of we are. We are going to the movies.

where = in or to what place or position. "where do you live?"

"I'm glad that I'm not where he is." May refer to a place, in trouble, or of the mind.

whether, weather (5)

whether = one or the other. Whether it's good or bad depends . . .

weather = climate, cold, hot, snowing. Oh! The weather outside is frightful. . .

who, whom (30)

he = who.

Is he going? Who is going?

him = whom.

Are you writing to him? To whom are you writing to?

To whom it may concern. Address when we don't know the persons name.

witch, which (18)

witch = an old lady that flies around on a broom.

which = basically, it's trying to decide between two or more objects, persons or actions.

I can't decide WHICH dress I should wear to the prom, and WHICH guy I should go with.

I can't decide WHICH would be more fun, sky diving or water rafting.

wondering, wandering (35)

"Is the killer known and wondering the streets?"

wondering = desire or be curious to know something.

wandering = traveling aimlessly from place to place.

wright, right (46)

The author stated. "Dam Wright."

wright = a wright is a maker or builder.

He said that a builder built a dam, I guess. Or was he trying to agree with the comment and meant, "Damn right!"

right = means correct (in this context).

right, can also mean which side? Or direction.

Your right hand; it's on the right side of the street; take a right at the end of the road.

write, right (7)

write = putting pen to paper making words. Write a letter.

Right = correct, opposite of wrong; direction, turn right at the light.

you're, your (1)

you're = contraction of you are; you're not smart, you are not smart.

your = possessive. Your mother wears army boots.

Add your own problem words here.

1. _____

_____

2. _____

_____

3. _____

_____

4. _____

_____

5. _____

_____

TWO

Punctuation

Commas are like darts.
Most never know where they will land
in a sentence or on the board.

Punctuation

There are four basic punctuation, the period, the exclamation mark or point, the question mark, and the comma.

While writing and you have to stop and take a breath = comma.

You have to stop, take a breath, and think what you're going to say next = period.

If you're screaming in your mind at or about something = exclamation mark.

If your sentence is in the form of a question = question mark.

An exclamation and question mark may be used in the middle of a sentence. They are, however, hardly ever used in this manner.

The best and probably the easiest way to learn punctuation is while reading, don't just read the words, but also the punctuation.

The Comma

The lowly comma, but so important for our breathing, is the most important of all the punctuation marks. Sometimes what appears to be simple is complicated and what appears to be complicated is simple. The first statement, I believe, defines the comma.

Webster's dictionary defines the comma as a "pause, interval."

You wouldn't say, "pause interval" as one doesn't define the other. If you said "fat person," fat describing the person, then you wouldn't use a comma. If you separate fat and person by a comma, "fat, person," "fat" would have no meaning in a sentence.

My (earlier) definition, "While writing and you have to stop and take a breath = comma," pretty much describes, "pause, interval."

"used to separate words or groups of words in a sentence"

I like apples, oranges, pears and peaches.

I like red apples, navel oranges, big pears and juicy peaches.

As the "and" separates pears and peaches you don't need a comma after "pears."

But, if you use the Oxford style, then a comma is required before the "and." The Oxford comma is popular among formal writers. You never use a comma before the "and" if there are only two items. A series requires three or more.

The Period

You have to stop, take a breath, and think what you're going to say next = period. (.)

The period like the exclamation point and the question mark not only ends the sentence, but it also ends your thought.

The Exclamation Point

"If you're screaming in your mind at or about something = exclamation mark." (!).

To express a strong feeling. Cool!

The Question Mark

If your sentence is asking a question = question mark. (?).

But not if it's an exclamation. If the sentence is in the form of an exclamation, then use an exclamation mark and not a question mark.

Where are you going? Is that your car?

Did the giant eat the fair maiden or did she manage to escape his grasp and flee to the castle where the prince saved her? Not all sentences in the form of a question needs to be short.

The Apostrophe

"I am reminded of a scene in Woody Allen's *Small Time Crooks* when . . . Hugh Grant offers to help ignoramuses Allen and Tracey Ullman with any sort of cultural education. 'Is there anything you want to know?' . . . And Allen says reluctantly, 'Well, I would like to know how to spell Connecticut.' What a great line that is. *I would like to learn how to spell Connecticut.* If you've similarly always wanted to know where to use an apostrophe, it means you *never will*, doesn't it? If only because it's so extremely easy to find out." – *Eats, Shoots & Leaves*, Lynne Truss.

To show possession

Here we have two types of nouns: singular and plural. Singular means only one and plural means two or more. Nouns identify a person, place or thing. Whether it's a proper noun, regular noun or a pronoun, it's a noun. The first four rules are lumped together here for easier understanding. Ask yourself first whether it's a singular or a plural noun.

For singular nouns:

For ALL (I didn't say, once-in-a-while, I said ALL) singular nouns add an apostrophe and an s; ('s).

my mother (you only have one mother; therefore, it's a singular noun).

my mother's dress; the teacher's assignment; the club's rules.

It doesn't matter whether the singular noun ends in an s. Add ('s).

The name Charles ends with an s, but it's a singular noun; therefore, you add an apostrophe and an s ('s).

Charles's. Dickens's novels. There is only one Dickens so it's singular.

No need to question this as it's the rule. If you don't like it - too bad.

Note: It is becoming acceptable in informal writing to merely add an apostrophe after singular words ending in s, without adding another s, but not in formal writing.

For plural nouns:

If the noun doesn't have an s, give it one. men, a plural noun, doesn't have an s, so give it one, men's, ('s).

If the noun ends in s, then just add the apostrophe. A lounge that belongs to the students, the students' (') lounge. Do not add another s.

In a capsule:

Singular nouns ALWAYS add 's.

Plural nouns that doesn't have an s, add an 's. If it already ends in s, then just add an apostrophe.

Possessive pronouns:

Words that already signify possession doesn't take an apostrophe. My, mine, our, ours. his, her, hers, their, theirs, its, your, yours.

Plurals

Plurals of numbers. "We have several size 12's in the back room."

Plurals of letters. "What has four i's but can't see?"

Abbreviated dates:

I was in Korea in '54.

The early 1900's.

(Answer: Mississippi has four i's but can't see.)

Possessive compounds

When you refer to two persons and each own their own item then you add apostrophe s ('s) after both names.

John's and Henry's watches were both stolen. (They each had a watch).

When both are co-owners of one item then only use apostrophe s ('s) after the last name.

John and Henry's business went bankrupt. (They both owned the one business). (One item for both, one apostrophe).

Possessive for indefinite pronouns

I love the English language, (sometimes). An indefinite pronoun is one that is not definite. It does not refer to any specific person, thing or amount—it is vague. All, another, any, anybody/anyone, anything, each, everybody/everyone, everything, few, many, nobody, none, one, several, some, somebody/someone, are indefinite pronouns. (Google search).

What I do is nobody's business. Certainly not talking about a specific person.

The police searched everyone's house, but not mine. Could be two houses or 20 houses. Indefinite amount of houses.

Miscellaneous expressions

(Don't sweat this one too much. If you know the others this one pretty much comes naturally by the sound of the speech).

a dollar = singular - 's. A dollar's worth.

ten dollars = plural - s'. Ten dollars' worth.

Ellipsis

The traditional usage of the ellipsis has generally been with 3 periods, with spaces between word and the first period, between each period, and a space between the next word. Word . . . word.

Used to show a pause. I . . . ah . . . yeah.

To show omitted words, sentences, and even whole sections of a speech when you feel that they would not add to or detract from the basic information you're trying to convey.

"The weather, despite being overcast, and threatening to downpour at any moment, cooperated." This statement could be shortened to: "The weather . . . cooperated."

At the end of a sentence to let your thought drift off, letting the reader to finish your thought.

For an in-depth analysis, google Wikipedia's definition.

Semicolon

a. The semicolon (;) is bigger than a comma, but smaller than a period, and may be used to join two independent clauses. An independent clause may also stand alone as a sentence.

b. If the independent clauses are so closely related as to subject, then I like to use a semicolon instead of making two separate sentences.

c. When two independent clauses are joined by a coordinate conjunction.

Conjunctive adverbs: also, as a result, for example, however, therefore, instead.

Ex.: I was late for work this morning; however, I did have a good excuse.

d. Used to separate groups that are separated by commas.

The meal consisted of soup and crackers; fish, steak; carrots, asparagus, and squash; for dessert, pies and cakes.

Using only commas wouldn't allow one to understand the different courses in the meal.

e. May also be used if the sentence is long and contain commas.

Quotation marks

Quotation marks are used to set off words in a sentence that is either spoken or quoted.

As per, my mother's favorite quote was from Shakespeare: "This above all, to thine own self be true."

"Charlie to Sam ' Don't climb that tree, Mr. Tanguay will kick you in the a—'."

Now as you can see in the previous sentence, my on-line student used two different types of quotation marks. When quoting what someone else tells a third party you would use a single quotation mark as opposed to a double quotation mark.

Quotation marks also set off the titles of things that do not normally stand by themselves: short stories, poems, and articles.

"To Try Men's Souls," is a book about Washington's attack on Trenton; on Christmas Eve.

Usually, a quotation is set off from the rest of the sentence by a comma.

The doctor said, "Take two of these pills every four hours."

The colon

Basically the colon is used to introduce a list of items.

Favorite high school sports are: football, baseball and soccer.

After a salutation. Dear Mr. So-and-So:

Between numerals. 9:00 am.

For other uses go to: (here I've introduced a web site).

http://www.thepunctuationguide.com/colon.html

The @ sign

The at symbol (@) is very familiar to anyone who has ever sent an email, as it is an integral component of an email address. Aside from its use in the aforementioned, the at sign is also used in price lists for commodities. It is also used in accounting and invoicing to mean "at the rate of." Various computer programming languages use the @ symbol. Originating as a scribe's shorthand method of writing the Latin word "ad," which means at, @ has been in use for centuries.

Slash/backslash\

Slash (/) = Mostly we see it in its and/or function.

The slash should be used to indicate characteristics of a single entity, either together

(the and function of the slash) or separately (the or function).

His apartment functioned as a bedroom/workshop. (Single entity).

He had just one room and it served a dual function.

It can be used for separate entities if they are part of a whole or closely related.

Make sure to order audio/visual equipment . . . . (Separately).

Used in dates: 09/03/2015.

Although, in the following example, not necessary to use his/her, he/she when an antecedent is present many people do use it. A person is . . . when he/she doesn't . . . .

Don't use the slash if writing it out will be clearer to your reader.

Backslash (\) = Generally only used in computer programming language.

(Sources: UNM college of education & the author. [the author is me]).

Note: See how the bracket is used to separate one thought from the main thought within the enclosed area?

Hyphen, dash (en & em)

hyphen = hyphens are used to join two words or parts of words together while avoiding confusion. run-down. up-to-date. And numbers, twenty-four, seventy-seven. To split a word between two lines of text.

Sometimes a hyphenated word, due to its common usage, loses its hyphen, e.g., e-mail is now email.

dash = Dashes can be used to add parenthetical statements or comments in much the same way as you would use brackets. Dashes can be used to create emphasis in a sentence. Use brackets in formal writing.

Example: You may think she is a liar - she isn't. (en dash).

En dash equals the space of a capital N.

Em dash equals the space of a capital M. That is why they are called en and em dashes.

The em dash is twice the width of the en dash. As a printer's devil these spaces were very important to me - for proper spacing—to start a paragraph and spacing between words—when typesetting for the newspaper. (I used the em dash to emphasize why the spacing is different). The hyphen is located on the upper line between 0 and = on your keyboard. Dashes are not included but by using two hyphens—without spaces between the words, the two hyphens automatically turn into an em dash.

Word word word word—word word word—word word word.

To use the en dash the easier way is to merely use a hyphen.

Parentheses/Bracket:

Common understanding of the parentheses and brackets is that they are the same thing, with the same usage. This is not necessarily true.

A parentheses, originating from Greek "the act of placing, to insert to the side" is an amplifying or explanatory word, phrase, or sentence inserted in a passage, which when removed, does not change the structure of the sentence.

A parentheses mark "()" is used to enclose a parentheses. In the example "The Blue sky (still with a touch of gray) was nice to see after a week of rain." clearly states that, when removing the parentheses, the Blue sky was nice to see. Without the parentheses marks "The Blue sky, still with a touch of gray, was nice to see after a week of rain." implies that some remaining gray aided in the appearance of the sky. The words in both examples are identical, but only the parentheses clarifies without altering the main sentence.

A bracket is one of a pair of marks [] used in writing and printing to enclose or separate, but not necessarily an amplifying or explanatory word, phrase, or sentence inserted in a passage. They are used to explain or comment on the quotation. "Joe called out 'Fred, [His name was actually Frank] where are you?'." Brackets are interruptions. When we see them, we know they've been added by someone else.

The bracket is also used as a parentheses mark when placing a parentheses inside a parentheses.

"The Children were playing all sorts of games (Hopscotch, jumping jacks, and [their own version of] patty cakes) until the parents called them home."

A bracket is a punctuation mark, a parentheses is a parentheses.

Note: There are seven more punctuation marks which are seldom, if ever, used. To see the complete list go to the word punctuation in the dictionary.

In days of yore
When writing first began,
There was no spacing between the words
And no punctuation marks.

I believe that
Many people still think
That they haven't been invented yet.

CHAPTER THREE

Be A Perspicacious Reader

How do you say

perspicacious

perspi(ration) + kay + (suspi)cious = perspi-ca-cious.

"Only 4% of those at the highest reading level are in poverty, but 43% of those at the lowest reading level are. . . . And you are much more likely to be in prison if you're illiterate or barely literate."—Writing Clear Paragraphs." Sixth Edition.

Introduction

What is it? It's picking up a book, a magazine, or a newspaper. Today we have Kindle, whatever that is. I like the fact that it not only opens one's mind but also opens the world. It's relaxing. It calms the heart and nerves.

Why do I believe it's important? Because it civilizes people. It gives one more interesting friends as you become a better conversationalist. It lets you use big words like "conversationalist." It helps you to become a better writer, which may allow you to write books and articles that are published in international magazines.

Or just becoming a better blogger. It helps you to advance faster at work, which means more money.

Reading brings you a better life style.

Definition

Perspicacious: of acute mental vision or discernment. – Merriam-Webster's, Collegiate Dictionary. Eleventh Edition.

To understand what the writer is trying to say. What his major point is. Recently I posted a run-on sentence as a humorous example of punctuation. Several readers turned it into a political discussion – not very discerning.

Cambridge Dictionaries: quick in noticing, understanding. If you don't understand what you're reading why are you reading it?

A keen reader. Able to read between the lines. To pick up the signature of the author. Able to pick up the inflections and nuances in the story.

A reader who doesn't pick up a book without also picking up a dictionary. One who doesn't bypass words that he doesn't know the definition of.

Which definition is the author using? Read all the definitions attributed to the word. How many are there? Which will you pick that will make sense in the story? Many times looking up synonyms will enhance your understanding of the definition.

Types

Although there are many styles and types of writings, I'll merely mention two.

If you have no reason to read . . . why read?

If your read is instructional, then you should have pen and paper on hand for taking notes. These will help you to review at a later date: to write a paper, or take a test.

(I have notes and stickies all over my books that helped me write this page).

Pleasure reading gives me the most satisfaction; but, it doesn't mean reading only "Harlequin Romances." Pleasure reading puts me in a *nether world,* oblivious as to what's above or around me. History, War, Politics, even books on grammar. I'm reading a book on punctuation, their usages and history called *Eats, Shoots & Leaves,* by Lynne Truss. I'm almost finished: then what? Oh! Then I'll be able to read *The Blue Book of Grammar and Punctuation,* by Jane Straus.

Flags of Our Fathers, by James Bradley. WWII, Iwo Jima. *Glory Road,* by Bruce Catton. The Civil War between the states. *The Christmas Sweater, by Glen Beck.*

To Try Men's Souls, by Newt Gingrich & William R. Forstchen. (My all time favorite). Revolutionary War. Washington's attack on Trenton. If you only have time for one more book before you die, then that's the one to read.

In my Series on Writing, I state that to become a good writer you must first become a good reader. All famous writers were or are avid readers.

The perspicacious reader never can walk away from his readings; as his new found knowledge, wonderful stories, and fantasies are forever embedded in his mind.

Inflections

The only way to appreciate the inflections of the author is by observing and understanding the punctuation, and how a word is used. You should, by now, have knowledge of most of the punctuation marks, their usages and how they change the tone of the story. This was all spelled out in chapter two: Punctuation.

Punctuation examples

Hello. (Merely a general greeting).

Hello! (Exclamation showing that, "I'm happy to see you," or nice surprise).

Hello? (In the form of a question, meaning. "Who's there?")

What does the word mean?

The vet (veteran) went to the VA hospital, but the staff was too busy to see him.

The vet (veterinarian) was able to save the dog.

The Secretaries of States did not vet (do a background check) the candidates.

Conclusion

"I declare after all there is no enjoyment like reading! How much sooner one tires of any thing than of a book!

When I have a house of my own, I shall be miserable if I have not an excellent library."— Jane Austen, Pride and Prejudice.

There is nothing comparable to owning a book. It's a present that you can open many times; but the best part is that I can do whatever I want with it. I can put stickies on pages that I want to refer back to, highlight passages that I want to re-read, and even write in the margins. When I re-read a passage and come across that-word-again, I don't have to look it up—again; I just look in the margin for the definition. A close second to owning is the borrowing from the library. Imagine! Thousands and thousands of books at my disposal—for free—it doesn't get much better than that.–The author.

If one never quotes another,
Then
He is not well read.

FOUR

Improving Your Writing

What is a sentence?

The first word starts with a capital letter,
It contains a subject and a predicate,
It conveys a complete thought, and
Ends with a punctuation.

Improving Your Writing

Introduction

". . . there are days when the result is so bad that no fewer than five revisions are required. In contrast, when I'm greatly inspired, only four revisions are needed." Writer John Kenneth Galbraith.

If such a famous writer has to re-write and proofread his writings so many times, why do we think that we won't look ignorant to our readers when we just post our writings without first proof reading?

Spelling

Spelling is always a problem. As we re-read what we wrote, our mind sees the word spelled correctly as it did the time we wrote it. Your mind thinks and writes, "I went out yesterday and shot a deer." But you wrote, "I went out yesterday and shut a deer." Reading it over quickly you may not pick it up—as I said earlier—as your mind is still reading "shot."

One way to avoid the trick your mind plays on you is to read the sentence backwards focusing on each word individually.

deer, a, shut – "shut, how did that get in there." "I didn't go out and shut a deer yesterday." So then you'd make the correction before you Post.

Percolating

The obvious subject in the writing series sequence would be word usage. As one should, though, before writing, is to let the ideas percolate in his mind. Like a percolator coffee pot percolates one gulp of water at a time, so should your ideas come to your mind—one gulp at a time. Allowing your mind to take one gulp of an idea at a time—percolating the ideas in your mind.

Once you have the concept of how your story is taking shape then you'll more easily be able to put it on paper. Let it percolate. If it doesn't compute; then it probably wasn't worth putting the idea down on paper.

This process doesn't speak to the procedures that are to follow to the conclusion of your story, but to the procedure before you even start to write.

Even in short, informal statements that I Post, or answer to one, on Facebook, I sit back and allow my mind to percolate the ideas; even if it's only for a moment.

Articles for publication or when I wrote Treatises, of course, I would, sometimes, let it percolate in my mind for days or weeks.

Sometimes you don't have the luxury of all the time you would like, but then you have to just suck-it-up, and do it.

Years back I was asked to write up a procedure, that I perfected, for publication in an international magazine. The problem was that he had to leave Connecticut at noon the next day to get to the publisher in New York in time for their 3:00 o'clock deadline. When he showed up at my office at noon the next day, the article was finished, he got to NY in time and my article was published. Months later while talking to an instructor from another state, he asked me if I'd seen that article in that magazine. I told him yes, "I wrote it."

Word usage

In spelling, I said to read the sentence backwards; but will this work for word usage? The only way is to continually study the 50+1 in chapter one and whether you read the sentence backwards or forwards you must pause at each of those combinations, and reflect upon whether you chose the right one.

It's, its; where, wear; you're, your; they're, their, there; etc. If upon reflection you're still not sure then go to your dictionary and verify which word to use. Also, by reading the synonyms, it will tell you which is the right word to use.

"But this will take time?" You might ask. I ask, "What is your hurry to prove to your intended readers that you're a dunce?"

Punctuation

As in Word Usage, I stated that that subject was well covered and you should refer to them when you run across any of the combinations. Punctuation, the 15 parts, has already been well covered.

Also stated in past comments, to become a better writer you must become a critical reader. Included in this type of reading is also reading the punctuation. When you proofread your article, don't just read the words, but also the punctuation. Whenever you come across a punctuation, stop and analyze it. Ask yourself, "Is this punctuation being used properly?" After a while it will come as second nature and the pause at each mark will be minor and won't interfere with your writing or enjoyment of reading.

"I love to shoot my family and dog." OR
"I love to shoot, my family, and dog."

"Let's eat grandma." OR
"Let's eat, grandma."

Capitalization

Major points:

Capitalize the first word of a sentence.

Capitalize proper nouns. Person's names, cities and states, and things. Chevrolet, but not car.

Referring to a deity. God, but not gods in general.

Starting a dialogue within a sentence. And then he said, "Get thee to a nunnery."

Titles and organizations. Lt., PhD, NRA, President Trump, but not talking about presidents in general.

"When in doubt, check it out." What does that mean? It means use a dictionary once in a while.

Grammar

Consisting of three parts:

a.   Subject and verb agreement.

b.   Pronoun and antecedent agreement.

c.   (1). Sentence fragments.

       (2). Rambling.

       (3). Run-on sentences.

a.   **Subject and verb agreement.**

The Basic Rule

A singular subject takes a singular verb.

The fleet, consisting of 12 ships, is in port.
Fleet is the subject, not ships.
As there is only one fleet, one being singular, you'd use a singular verb: is.
You wouldn't say, "The fleet are in port."

A plural subject takes a plural verb.

The 12 ships are out to sea due to the predicted typhoon.
Ships is the subject, which is plural; therefore the verb is plural: are.

(Believe me! You don't want to be in port when a typhoon hits. Out to sea, you can either outrun it or ride it out. Luckily we were able to outrun one out of Hong Kong).

The Basic Rule is just that, the basic rule. There are 10 specific rules.

b.   Pronoun, antecedent agreement

An antecedent is the noun that the pronoun refers to or replaces." – Write Source 2000, @734.

All pronouns have antecedents. (Whether you can find it or not).

All pronouns must agree with their antecedents in number, person and gender.

A person (noun/antecedent) is guilty of . . . if he (pronoun) enters unlawfully. . . .

In the above sentence it appears that the pronoun and antecedent do not agree.

But they do.

When the antecedent is an indefinite noun (person) then there is no gender conflict. You do not define the pronoun (he), but you define the antecedent/noun (person). A person includes both males and females; therefore, in the above sentence females are also included and can be charged with the crime.

An occasional use of the two gender pronouns, he/she is acceptable, but an overuse sounds laborious.

Number: <u>Everyone</u> is singular so <u>he</u> or <u>she</u> is correct, not they.
Person: Refers to <u>people</u>, not animals or inanimate objects.
Gender: <u>Male</u> and/or <u>female</u>.

For a more in-depth study refer to your five grammar books and the dictionary.

(You do have five grammar books and a dictionary, don't you?)

c.   **Use clear, concise sentences**

A sentence starts with a capital letter, ends with a period, question mark, or an exclamation point, and conveys a complete thought; therefore, do not use sentence fragments, comma splices, run-on sentences, or ramble.

Sentence fragments = incomplete thoughts.

Usually occurs when you only have a phrase or dependent clause.
After the marathon ended. (Fragment).
After the marathon ended, we went home. (Complete thought).

Comma splice = connecting two complete sentences with a comma.
You try to connect two independent thoughts by a comma.

Run-on sentences = overuse of AND or OR.
The solution is to break it up into sentences.

Rambling = adding useless words or information.
Stay with the main topic. Superfluous facts only tend to confuse the reader.

Don't repeat the noun with a pronoun:

Incorrect: John and I, WE are going. (If you do, you're a tautologist).

Correct: John and I are going.

Conclusion

What is writing and why do we do it?

Writing is merely transferring what is in our minds to paper. We do it to convey these thoughts to others, or to preserve them for ourselves, as in a diary.

Most writers develop a signature; therefore, they can be identified by their style of writing. When my Yale, PhD. co-worker edited or proof-read my papers, he would not change them into his style, but would preserve my signature. This is important. Be yourself. Don't try to emulate another. People want to get to know you; not an Updike or a Twain.

The preceding paragraph doesn't mean boredom. You write in different styles to convey different meanings: convey information, humor, sarcasm, etc., while still maintaining your personal signature.

Use words that feel right for you. But certainly use a thesaurus to help you find a better word to get your point across. But once your writing is clear, natural and interesting—leave it alone. Write what you would like to read and what your readers would like to read.

Don't overuse the same writing technique in the same story. A hyperbole, a metaphor, a paradox, sarcasm, satire, a simile, or a synecdoche can get boring very quickly. But a few, here and there, can really spice up a story, so certainly use them, but don't overuse them. Stay away from overused cliques: quick as a fox, dumb as a rock, etc.

The only way to learn how to write well, is to write. When I taught "Report Writing for Criminal Justice Professionals," in college, I started, the very first day and minute, by giving a writing assignment. Here's how it went. "This is a writing course, so take out a piece of paper and pencil/pen. Clear your desk of everything else. There will be no talking or ask any questions during the assignment. Now when I say 'start', you will write for five minutes. Start." You should do this exercise often if you want to become a good writer. At first there was chaos, but later in the course the 10 minute exercises produced many wonderful, impromptu stories.

Not to be known as a dunce by your readers you should also follow the other suggestions in this book. Let the idea percolate in your mind before writing; then check your spelling, word usage, punctuation, capitalization, and grammar. You should be proud of what you write, or why write at all.

Sources:

Report Writing for Criminal Justice Professionals by Larry S. Miller and John T. Whitehead PhD.

Merriam-Webster's, Collegiate Dictionary - Eleventh Edition

Write Source 2000, A Guide to Writing, Thinking & Learning, P. Sebranek, V. Meyer, D. Kemper

Writing Clear Paragraphs, Sixth Edition, R. Donald, J. Moore, B. Morrow, L. Wargetz, K. Werner

The Blue Book of Grammar and Punctuation, 11th Edition, Jane Straus, L. Kaufman, T. Stern

Eats, Shoots & Leaves, The Zero Tolerance Approach to Punctuation, Lynne Truss

www.GrammarBook.com, Free Online English Usage Rules

FIVE

Thinking

"Rarely do we find men who willingly
engage in hard, solid thinking.
There is an almost universal quest for easy
answers and half-baked solutions.
Nothing pains some people more than having to think."
—Martin Luther King, Jr.

Introduction

It's apparent by the Posts on Facebook and other venues that many people do not think. Spewing out the first thing that comes to mind, whether verbally or in writing, does not constitute thinking. Thinking is a complex endeavor and if at the end of the process it is to be shared with others, it must be a complete, comprehensive, and understandable by the listener or reader.

One cannot say, as many do, that as long as I understand what I want to convey it is sufficient. It is not sufficient for the listener or the reader. If you're a sloppy writer then you're a sloppy thinker . . . which is not thinking at all.

But not all thinking must be for the benefit of others. Private thinking for one's self, such as in meditation; trying to decide on a future course of action; and spending time thinking about a loved one, deceased or far away, that you miss, can certainly be a pleasant thinking experience.

Thinking is not merely letting thoughts run helter-skelter through the mind . . . it requires a process.

Process: a particular course of action intended to achieve a result.

The Process

Process: a particular course of action intended to achieve a result . . . formulating ideas in the mind.

To properly think, one's mind must be healthy, but although a young person's mind may be healthy doesn't mean that he or she will think rationally. The mind must also be mature.

The maturity of the mind is far different than the maturational level of the individual and each person develops his thinking maturity at different ages. The mind is basically wired by the age of three; although some changes can be made to age five.

But no matter at what age, the thinking process should lead to some rational conclusion. Unfortunately, that is not always the case. For teenagers, in many situations, the action comes before the thinking, or said another way, he reflects on what he did, not having thought about what he's going to do. Thinking did not precede the irrational behavior.

Another thought process that skews your thinking is rationalization or self-delusion. In order to avoid unpleasant thoughts or behaviors one rationalizes them away by making excuses. Although a very common way of thinking it does not lead to the truth or to a proper conclusion of the process.

Rationalization or self-delusion is not always a negative. When a truth or experience is so grievous that delving/thinking on it may lead to depression would be understandable for the preservation of the sanity of the mind.

Don't Be A Bad Thinker

I was talking to a gentleman at the recycling center the other day about thinking. How did that happen, you might ask. He asked how I was, so I told him that my newest Series on Thinking was somewhat difficult. He said, "My wife is an over-thinker." What a wonderful (non) word to describe one that thinks out a problem to the degree that a solution is hardly ever reached. I then got his name, Edison Walker, and later thanked him for engaging in the following dialogue that helped me write this page.

Further discussion allowed me to come up with my own (non) word. "The under-thinker." People who make snap decisions based on incomplete data generally find that the results are unsatisfactory.

An example used during our discussion was that of someone building a structure. We assumed that the structure would require 400 nails for it to be a sound structure. The under-thinker uses 40 nails as he's in too big of a hurry. The first strong wind then blows his structure down. The over-thinker, on the other hand, is going to use 4,000 nails, just to be positive, but then the structure never gets finished. Both forms of thinking are equally as bad.

Then, we come to the "in-the-middle-thinker." In my Series on "Improving Your Writing," I discuss that before putting anything down on paper one should let the idea percolate in the mind. That's what thinking is. The successful thinker takes his time, allows the thoughts to percolate in his mind, one thought at a time. Thoughts come to us not in a tsunami, but like water in a gentle stream.

That is why we must give it time for all the thoughts to come together, like the percolating coffee pot to finish, resulting in a pleasant tasting cup of coffee. Once the process is completed then take action. It doesn't mean that the result will always be perfect, and there is nothing wrong with tweaking it a bit later on, as the way Mr. Walker put it; to continue the process/thinking to the final satisfactory result.

Slow It Down

It would seem paradoxical to say that, "If I slow down my thinking it will save me time."

If I rush my thinking, usually I will make a bad decision, and therefore, I will most probably have to rethink and do the task all over again. It can be compared to the carpenter's way of doing a project. All good carpenters know to, "measure twice, cut once." It's a lot faster to think/measure twice than to have to cut another board. Wasting one's time, re-cutting the board, or to redo the project.

Always in a hurry and not thinking it out, like 'Tim the Tool Man Taylor' causes more accidents. The carpenter who doesn't secure his board or doesn't take the time to put the guard on the blade is prone to accidents–like Tim. Putting all the proper thoughts into play will allow one to be safer. Improper thinking while driving leads to over two million catastrophes each year.

Thinking doesn't necessarily mean that it can only be used to lead to a physical project, but also may lead to a conclusion in the mind. An incident may have happened that upset you. By thinking through the steps of the incident, you may determine that it wasn't such a bad thing after all and then just let it pass. This type of thinking clears the mind of negatives. Allowing too many negative thoughts to occupy your mind may lead to a mental health problem.

To solve problems, to make decisions about the future, what to have for dinner, and a hundred other reasons, but, usually, if you think too quickly, you will not be satisfied with the end result.

And why not think for sheer pleasure! Just letting your mind to slowly think pleasant thoughts to soothe your heart and soul can be a most enriching pass time; as I alluded to in the Introduction.

Types

Thinking is difficult enough without having to think about thinking so one can write about thinking. (But here I am).

The type of intelligence our mind possesses will determine how we think also.

Some say that there are nine types of intelligence, others say there are seven, and still others say there are two; which are listed below.

(Gf) Fluid intelligence.

Fluid intelligence or fluid reasoning is the capacity to reason and solve novel problems, independent of any knowledge from the past.

(Gc) Crystallized intelligence.

Crystallized intelligence is the ability to use learned knowledge and experience.

Everyone has some of both, but to what degree. The inventor certainly thinks differently than the mechanic who learned his trade in a technical college, or on the job.

Every one should analyze how they think. When thinking about a task, don't merely think about the task, but also how your mind worked to come to the conclusion. Once you understand how your mind works you won't be wasting time by allowing your mind to wander. This will allow you to stay on task, causing quicker and better results.

The least productive way to think is with a closed mind. Once you've become an ideologue you've basically stopped thinking. You are able to continue your profession, such as acting or fixing cars, but at this point you're merely a robot.

Conclusion

"The action of using one's mind to produce thoughts."—Webster's Dictionary.

"To produce," as in the production of a car. A car has many parts and your mind has many many thoughts. The car manufacturer produces cars while your mind produces thoughts.

Each part of the car is a separate entity as each thought is a separate entity. As the parts, like your thoughts, come together you have a finished product.

Only if the parts, like your thoughts, are properly assembled will the manufacturer have a usable car and you'll have a usable solution.

The more you use your mind, the easier it will be for you to solve complex problems and tasks.

CHAPTER
SIX
Listening

Listening to the voice of a friend,
Is not only music to ones ear
But it also takes away loneliness.

Introduction

Listening is not the same as: Hearing.

Hearing is the sense through which a person or animal is aware of sound. Hearing is merely one of the five senses: sight, hearing, taste, smell, and touch.

Listening, on the other hand, is to hear something with thoughtful attention. The sound you hear means something to you.

We hear many sounds that we don't pay attention to; therefore, we aren't listening. A plane flies overhead; a car driving on the highway; the noise in a public place, such as in a shopping mall; we hear these sounds, but they don't mean anything to us at the time . . . so are we listening?

Listening is not merely a sense like hearing, but a skill. Unfortunately most people have never perfected the art of listening.

Is it our fault? Probably not. Have you ever taken, or even heard about, a course in any school titled, *Listening 101?*

Sounds

You hear with your ear and listen with your mind. (The author).

As I stated in the Introduction, there are many sounds that we don't pay attention to; therefore, we don't listen to them. But if we ignore all sounds we'd be doing ourselves a great disservice, as many sounds are even more pleasing than the human voice.

You hear a plane overhead. Do you listen to it? Probably not, but as a former pilot I do. As I listen to the sound of the motors they tell me that things are fine and that the probability is great that the pilot, and his passengers, will reach his destination and land safely. Having crashed a plane myself, knowing that that pilot is OK makes me feel good.

What is it about a baby breathing, snuggled against his young mother's breast? His mother hears the breathing, but I'd venture a guess that she's also listening. If the breathing sounds normal, not labored, it's probably the most pleasing sound that a mother can hear.

"Listen to that." One birdwatcher says to another. "Can you identify what kind of bird that is?" What they are doing is listening. Listening for the sound that will give them much pleasure. What have these people acquired by their activity? They have developed their listening skills . . . I envy them.

Back from her trip my wife didn't see or hear any hummingbirds off of our back deck. Of course I didn't keep their feeder up, and she, therefore, thought that I probably killed them all. After cleaning and putting in new sugared-water, they returned. Sitting on the back deck, waiting, the singing noise of their little wings, I could see her joy that the little ones had returned.

I heard them . . . she listened.

Silence

One of the better ways to learn to listen is to listen to silence. Each day for 10-15 minutes we should pick a quiet spot in our surroundings and listen . . . to the silence.

During this time you won't be able to interrupt as no one is talking to you. You won't be trying to formulate an answer, which you think is far more important than what another is saying; because no one is saying anything.

You might ask, "how can I listen to silence." Have you never said or heard, "this silence is deafening," or "this silence is driving me crazy."

Of course those statements are not true, but they merely confirm that we live in a noisy world. One that rarely allows our mind any peace. What if we embraced silence for a few minutes a day? We could then start to listen to nature; to ourselves; to a deceased parent; to a special friend that we've spent many hours in conversation with, re-listening to some of their stories that you enjoyed so much; and sometimes . . . the word of God.

Just looking at a picture of a loved one, deceased or merely far away, many times, if you listen real close, you'll hear them speak. These are the most soothing ways to listen: both to the mind and heart.

Alternatives

Listening to your favorite music: Many years ago on Sunday afternoons I'd lie in bed and listen to the Boston Symphony on the radio. The music would carry me on its sound waves to another place.

Listening to something exciting: McCarthy's voice announcing the Joe Lewis fights would get my excitement up. Back in the '40's I'd never miss a Joe Lewis fight. Late at night, in a dark bedroom, I'd listen to every word describing the fight. You just knew there would be a knockout, but when would it come, which round! 70 fights, 66 wins, 52 knockouts.

Meditation: Listening to your inner voice. Your inner voice speaks to you often. Have you ever heard it? Have you ever listened to it? If you truly listen, it will tell you exactly who you are.

Prayer: Although praying seems to do more with talking than listening, the peacefulness of the endeavor also allows you to listen between your prayers.

Reading: If you read between the lines, or is it listen between the lines. In the quietness you'll be able to figure out what the author's main plot is. His inferences, his nuances, his, his . . . what is he really trying to say.

Listening to something interesting: Listening to something that you're extremely interested in will make you a better listener. You will not interfere with the activity or allow any outside distractions.

Merely not talking for a while each day will make you a better listener.

Preconceptions & Roadblocks

Everyone listens through filters. These are based on our family background, education, morals, religion, etc. To become a better listener we must bypass our preconceptions.

We cannot ignore them completely, but by practice we can mostly set them aside. It doesn't mean that we will just take what the speaker is saying as Gospel truth, but that we will be better able to understand the point that the speaker is trying to make.

Are you more apt to pay closer attention (listen) to someone whose appearance is pleasing to the eye? Or someone who is sloppily dressed. A relative who you were told is a bore, or crude. Or one you were told is smart, went to college, and is attractive.

Preconceptions many times disappoint us. Have you ever changed your mind about a person after listening to him?

As a police officer I've had to listen to many types of persons, from the President of a University to the janitors. To crime victims where the most minor details may have

helped me solve the case. Where a missed piece of information may have caused serious injury or death to 20,000 people. Not just listening to words, but also listening between the words: what the speaker is actually trying to convey.

One major roadblock to listening is the environment. It's obvious that being in a public place with all the extraneous noises makes it harder to carry on a conversation, and to listen. It's not a pleasant listening experience when the other person has to shout. You know the difficulty, and therefore should keep the talking to a minimum and staying on more mundane topics. Unless it's an emergency, better to wait for a more quiet time and place to have a deep and personal conversation.

I promise, that soon, the posts will have to do with two people talking to each other, i.e., having a conversation. But, what good is a conversation if we're not listened to.

Talking Heads

Don't be a Talking Head. Many anchors and their guests on TV are the rudest and worst listeners on the planet. I suppose at three million dollars a year in salary, I probably wouldn't care about listening to anyone either.

But to their listening audience it's very disconcerting. None of them allows the other to finish his point, so all we, the listener get, is partial information and sound bites How rude. How disingenuous to their audience.

"Having said that." (I hate that phrase.) I know what you just said. As I'm a good listener. I remember from a second ago what you said. This thought may have been better stated in the Improving Your Writing chapter, but using trite, cute sayings usually turn off your listeners.

People listen in spurts which may last from a few seconds to a few minutes; but no one can listen with complete attention for a full hour. (Paraphrased from *Write Source 2000*).

Having used the suggested listening methods on the previous pages, you should, by now, be able to attentively listen for more than a few seconds. Listening actively will help you to listen. You do that by looking the speaker in the eyes and nodding your head. These gestures will keep you more focused and to listen more accurately.

Eventually, while listening, thoughts will come to mind. You may want a clarification, or you may have an idea to enhance the point that the speaker is making. These are fine, but you should not let these interfere with your listening. You should wait until there is an appropriate break, and then convey to the speaker that you have something that you'd like to say. If the speaker says, "Let me finish my point, then I'll be happy to listen to your idea." Then, let him finish.

After all, are you there to listen, to have a conversation, or to lecture? Don't be rude like the Talking Heads by constantly interrupting.

Why?

We listen to learn, for enjoyment, and friendship.

To a teacher in school to learn the subject matter. When listening for this reason we should have pencil and paper on hand so we can take notes. Note taking, though, is not writing down every word that is being said. Copious notes to help us remember what was said and then expand on them for further study to prepare for test-taking or to keep up with the new material. Any questions should be written down so not to forget; when you have a chance later to ask.

Listening to lectures. Listening to lectures can be broken down into two parts.

One reason may be to advance your knowledge about a subject; but the other may be for just pure enjoyment of listening to a good speaker or hearing about an interesting subject. I once went to a lecture given by Attorney F. Lee Bailey. He spoke for one hour and fifteen minutes, without notes, covered several points, and tied them all up in the last five minutes.

Being a member of the Criminal Justice system, it was quite an experience, and I tried to emulate his style when I lectured, i.e.., not to constantly refer to notes or teleprompters like many boring lecturers do. As I was invited to the after-lecture party, I was able to tell him how much I enjoyed it; as I know how it feels when you get positive feedback.

After one of my Child Abuse lectures a teacher told me, "You really bothered me today." Which I answered, "It's about time someone did." She then thanked me and left. After another, a young man, who had been abused as a child, told me that he fought against abusing his children every day. He thought that he was the only one with those feelings, and that my lecture would go a long way in helping him with his struggle.

Another pleasant experience was listening to Bishop Fulton J. Sheen, first on the radio and then television. He died in 1979 and his cause for canonization as a saint was officially opened in 2002.

And of course, one of the most pleasing of all . . . listening to a friend.

It's called a conversation. Listening to each other attentively cements a bond between you that grows stronger every time.

Listening, listening, listening. What more enjoyment can you get, other than by listening.

Conversation

"The most basic and powerful way to connect to another person is to listen." "Practicing the Sacred Art of Listening," by Kay Lindahl.

A conversation is listening to each other attentively. A conversation cements a bond between the conversant that grows stronger every time.

Attentively:

1. characterized by or giving attention; observant: an attentive audience.

2. thoughtful of others; considerate; polite; courteous: an attentive host.

If you hog the conversation, whether in a group or with just another person, you're giving a lecture and not having a conversation. Being thoughtful means to listen without interruption. Being attentive means that you don't just merely hear the other, as you can't wait for him to shut-up so you can get your ideas across. Being observant means that you're aware of the speakers physical movement and what they add to the words. Your demeanor is how you show your friend that you're paying attention, and that you're interested in what he's saying: by making eye contact, by not making annoying guttural sounds, and by not making fidgety body movements.

Be thoughtful means that when you've made the point or finished introducing the subject, then let the other acknowledge or add his idea to the conversation . . . conversation is a two-way street. In one of his performances, Jeff Dunham, the ventriloquist, was talking at the same time as his dummy Peanuts. Peanuts admonished him by saying, "You're a ventriloquist: I talk, you talk, I talk, you talk, that's it. Could anyone have described what a conversation is: better than Peanuts?

To be, or not to be, that is . . . Sorry! I just got carried away as sometimes when I pause in my writings, Hamlet's soliloquy to Ophelia comes to mind. (Having liked it—I memorized it).

To be involved in a truly meaningful conversation ask yourself, "What wants to be said next?" Not, "What do I want to say?" What wants to be said, comes from the soul, when what do I want to say, comes from the ego. Of course, not all conversations must be earth-shattering. Frivolous and lighthearted conversations can be very fulfilling too.

Only if all statements uttered are truthful for it to be a conversation. Call untruthful dialogue between two or more persons what you want, but it is not a conversation.

Once upon a time a woman called a friend and stated that she had had one of the best conversations of her life the other day. Thinking back, the friend realized that she had hardly said anything. . . . There's something very healing about being listened to.

Conclusion

In the paragraph, *Improving Your Writing*, I talk about allowing your idea(s) to percolate in your mind. This I have been doing for ever so long, and nothing seemed to formulate in my mind for the conclusion.

The problem is that I was thinking about, "What do I want to say," instead of, "What wants to be said." Finally, listening to my inner voice, "What wants to be said," came to me.

1. The most precious gift you can give a friend is to (truly) listen to them.

2. Parents worry or are concerned about their children: whether they will grow up properly, get a good education, have a good job, marry well, etc., but do not realize that all of these things will be happily taken care of by themselves . . . if you just listen to your child from birth. But, it is *never* too late to start.

You always put yourself in more danger
When you don't listen
To your Inner Voice.

SEVEN

Personal Safety Tips

Surviving an IED
(Improvised Explosive Device)

As the government won't, we should train ourselves to survive an IED.

Citizens of Israel are so well trained that an unattended bag or package would be reported in seconds by citizens who know to publicly shout,

"unattended bag"

the area would be quickly and calmly cleared by the citizens themselves.

If the spectators who saw the (explosive) backpacks unattended at the Boston Marathon had shouted the warning and the people close by knew what that meant, many would have quickly left the area and the injured would have been far less.

They announce this warning at airports, why not in the streets?

Introduction

This list is not all inclusive, but merely a guide for you to become more aware of and to start to enhance your personal safety.

The more you think about and follow these basic tips, the more tips you will think of on your own.

Do not hesitate to add your good ideas to the list based on your particular situation.

Safety Tips

1. Look outside before leaving the safety of the building you are in, whether your home, apartment or place of work, especially at night. Be more vigilant if you live or work in a less than perfect neighborhood.

2. Look around well ahead of you while you approach your car in a parking lot, street or detached garage. If you see a stranger or strangers loitering by your car which make you uncomfortable go back into the building.

    Note: If the building you work in have doors that lock automatically when they are shut. You won't be able to get back into the building to avoid any danger(s). In these situations you want to have security or a co-worker walk you to your car.

3. Before getting in your car look inside, especially the floor of the back seat, behind the back seat in a SUV, or the cargo area of a van.. Every time, even if after getting gas and going into the convenience store.

4. Have your keys ready so there is no unnecessary delay in getting into your car. You did lock your car when you left it, didn't you?

5. Lock your door as soon as you get in your car. If the location or situation makes you apprehensive drive away immediately. You can relocate the car across the parking lot or down the street to put on your seat belt, quickly, and drive away from the area.

6. Increase your awareness level several blocks before your destination. As you approach, observe whether the location is basically the same as always or do you see or hear something that makes you apprehensive. If so, do not stop but drive away and check the location a few minutes later.

   If the situation is the same, leave again and try to find a police officer, (cruiser) or go to a friend's house or a public area.

   If there is a person that you know at the destination, call to have him help you to determine whether the situation poses a danger or not.

7. Look around before you unlock the door and exit your vehicle. Do not exit until you feel reasonably safe. If the area makes you uncomfortable: drive away.

8. Don't stop on the highway for a stranger, even if he says something is wrong with your car. Drive to a police or gas station. Learn the sound of your car so if someone tries to flag you down, by telling you something is wrong, you will know whether he is trying to trick you into a compromising or dangerous situation. Of course you would stop for a real emergency, such as if your car was on fire.

You might agree that it was more important for me to learn and understand the sounds and quirks of the airplane I was flying than you with your car, but I believe it's just as important for you.

Whether anyone is trying to flag you down for criminal assault or whether you're just stranded out on some deserted highway, especially at night. If you had been able to identify, by sound, that something was wrong you might have stopped in a much safer place.

I have listened to the sound of my car every mile I've driven since flight school fifty-five years ago.

9. a. Don't let your guard down just because you're near your house or apartment. Continue to look around and listen until you are safely inside. Then, lock your doors. Do you have modern, adequate locks on your doors and windows?

    b. Another concern is for the safety of one that you are dropping off at their house. Don't just drive away. Wait until they are safely inside. I've always told the person to wave from inside or flick on/off the porch light. Young girls have been killed just outside their front door by someone hiding in the bushes. Overgrown bushes is a perfect hiding place.

    c. And of course you and your friend/co-worker are leaving work (seminar, college class, etc.) after working late and after dark. You peel out of the lot without any thought of your friend. His car doesn't start and he's stranded. If you're the last two, both should wait for the other and make sure that cars start. If his car is moving and behind you, it's running.

10. Listen to your "Inner Voice." This is the voice inside you telling you that something may be wrong. Call it what you will, experience, training, sixth sense, intuition or "Inner Voice" but don't ignore it.

The greater the perceived danger the louder the voice will be.

11. Consider carrying a personal protection device such as an aerosol pepper spray or mace if your situation warrants it.

   Do not put it on your key chain or in your purse. When the key is in the door or ignition you cannot use it and the purse is the first thing stripped away by a mugger. Carry it in your hand and next to you in the car.

   Wasp spray seems to work even better and quicker than mace or pepper spray. It is legal to own, is more accurate and shoots a distance of 20 feet.

   If you don't own a gun, obviously another kind of personal protection device, you should have a few of these around the house. Always familiarize yourself with such devices before you need it.

   Note: Verify the legality of carrying any such items with your local police department.

12. For victims of stalkers: (And people with unwanted admirers).

   a. If possible have security walk you to your car after work, especially at night.

   b. Try not to be alone. This means inside buildings also.

   c. Learn where the police departments are. Near your place of work, home and along your most raveled routes to and from work.

   d. Take different routes to and from work periodically.

e. Look in rear view mirrors more often for someone possibly tailing you. Try to remember cars that act peculiar. If you see it more than once, especially in the same location, it may be tailing you. Write down the registration number and notify the police.

f. If you think you're being tailed drive to the nearest police station or a public area. DO NOT drive off the highway onto some deserted side street, stay on the main arteries.

g. If your stalker or a suspicious person rear-ends your car, (usually on purpose), do not stop to exchange information. Drive to the nearest police station or public area, if your car is still operable, and notify the police. If your car is not operable, keep your doors locked, windows rolled up and sound the horn continuously. If you have a cell phone dial 911 in all suspicious situations. This may not be as prevalent today as he would deploy his airbag. When warranted you could back up into him and deploy them, but certainly not my first choice.

Disclaimer: The author does not accept any responsibility for your safety, that is your job. These 12 are merely tips to enhance your awareness. They are not all inclusive.

Note: For Driving and more Personal Safety Tips go to my web site. www.youarestupidif.com.

EIGHT

Jury Nullification

Nullification
What is this power
That
We freemen have?

As told to the jury;
"You have a right to take upon yourselves
to judge [both the facts and law]."
John Jay, first Chief Justice of the United States Supreme Court.

Jury Nullification

*Jury Nullification is the most powerful tool that
we have to preserve our freedom.*

Jury Nullification was introduced into America in 1735. It was the law in England for over 400 years. As subjects of the Crown we inherited it from them.

In 1779 it was codified into the 6th Amendment as part of the Bill of Rights of our Constitution.

A person charged with a crime has the right to a trial by a jury of his peers.

What good is this most powerful tool we have to preserve our freedom if we never put ourselves in the position to use it?

The only time one can use it is when he's on the jury. Why then do most people try to get off of jury duty? When you do, you're only helping to destroy your ability to remain free.

If you are ever charged with a crime wouldn't you like a true freedom-loving Patriot to be on your jury? Or would you be satisfied to merely have the ones who weren't able to avoid it.

Today you can go into a bar and have a drink without the risk of being arrested and jailed. Why? In the 1920's juries refused to convict anyone who were prosecuted for a liquor law violation. As prosecutors couldn't get a conviction, the law became unenforceable. This went a long way in overturning Prohibition.

Did the defendant violate the law? Yes, but a juror does not only have to consider the facts but also the law itself.

Judges, in their charge to the jury, may tell the jury that they can only consider the facts and rule based on his explanation of the law. He is a liar, and the juror doesn't have to follow his charge.

In fact, New Hampshire passed a law (2013) allowing the defense to tell the jury of this power: Jury Nullification. Although not codified two other states allow it, (Washington & Alaska).

A juror cannot be punished for his decision. (Settled case law). Should we not do the same today? If you think that the facts and/or the law itself makes no sense to you your vote is "Not Guilty."

Congratulations! You've decided to do your patriotic duty and show up for jury duty.

Now you're being questioned by the prosecutor, "Have you heard about Jury Nullification?" Here he wants you to say, if you did, yes, so he can kick you off the jury as they don't like independent minded jurors.

Of course if you have, you must say yes as you're under oath and could go to jail for five years for perjury if you say no.

But do not just say yes. "Yes I have, but I'm not an attorney. Could you please explain it to me so I'll have a legal understanding of it." Now he'll just drop it or better yet explain it.

Now, even if he excuses you, the rest of the jurors will know what it is. If not asked, you do not have to volunteer the information or mention to the other jurors that you've heard about it.

Jury Nullification is a power that you personally have. You don't run around town and holler, "I know about freedom of speech, I know about freedom of speech." Or, do you?

Enough history and background.

Usually when someone tries to sell an item or an idea, by the time they get to the point most people are asleep; therefore, let's get to the items when Jury Nullification should come into play.

1. If the law is, or you believe it is, unconstitutional.

2. If the facts do not match, or you believe that they do not match, the crime charged.

3. If the punishment, or you believe that the punishment, can or will be much greater than warranted for the action of the accused.

4. Shocks your conscience. "You don't have to leave your conscience at the courthouse door." (If you vote your conscience you'll never lose a night's sleep over your decision).

Note: Another area seldom mentioned is if you believe that the witness for the prosecution is lying.

A lawyer, whether the prosecutor or the defense attorney, is legally bound to never put on a witness that he believes may lie. If he does and is found out, he may be disbarred.

Now let's elaborate on these items when Jury Nullification should come into play.

1. "If the law is, or you believe it is, unconstitutional."

Several years ago Morton Grove, IL passed an ordinance that no one in the city could possess a gun.

The 2nd Amendment states otherwise, therefore unconstitutional. If you were on the jury where a female had a gun because she was afraid of an abusive ex-husband and was being prosecuted for a weapons charge, how would you vote? "Guilty," or "Not Guilty."

Connecticut passed a law that by Dec. 31, 2013 people had to register certain types of guns. Many did not. If one was prosecuted for that law, how would you vote? Do you believe that gun registration is unconstitutional?

Not only are many laws unconstitutional but many regulations are. Violating some of them carry jail time which are crimes and are treated as such; therefore, you should nullify those regulations also— by voting "Not Guilty."

2. "If the facts do not match, or you believe that they do not match, the crime charged."

Another way of looking at this section is, "Misapplication of the law."

A person moved into New Jersey and stayed with his sister until he could find a permanent place. He then moved from his sisters to his place within New Jersey. He was stopped by police who found guns in his car.

They misapplied the moving exception to the law. The prosecutor said that if he had come directly from out of state he would have been OK. What! You can't move within the state of NJ? He was convicted and given four years in prison. No state law says you have to leave your guns at the old house.

The law itself may be all right but the facts did not match the crime charged. Ignorance of the jury members cost this man four years in prison.

Note: The saddest part about this case is that the judge was duty bound to discard the jury's verdict, and vote "Not Guilty," but he did not.

A judge has the power to overturn a "Guilty" verdict but not a "Not Guilty."

3. "If the punishment, or you believe that the punishment, can or will be much greater than warranted for the action of the accused."

Here we aren't necessarily talking about the 8th Amendment, which in part, deals with cruel and unusual punishment.

In a 2013 case about an ex-felon who had served jail time several years before and who since got a job, married and had 4 children was suspected of a burglary. Upon searching his house they found some tools stolen from storage areas. Although the burglary charge was dropped the police found eight shotgun shells he acquired from a neighbor while helping her get rid of her deceased husband's effects. Hiding the shells so his children could not find them, he forgot about them.

Minimum mandatory sentence - 15 years for possession of the shells. He had never used a gun in the commission of or committed a crime of violence; he didn't even own a shotgun. (US v. Young).

Are you the one who was bragging to your fellow co-workers that you were able to get off of (his) jury duty?

California's "three strikes" law and other state's "minimum mandatory," imposes severe jail sentences for minor crimes. Many are serving "life imprisonment without possibility of parole" for minor offenses—drug or other non-violent crimes. Some punishments are harsher than for rape and murder.

The classic caricature of justice run amok is Inspector Javert in Victor Hugo's novel *Les Misérables*, pursuing Jean Valjean for stealing bread for hungry children. In that case, Valjean knew that he was breaking the law—Edward Young had no idea.

4. "Shocks your conscience."

In the context of Jury Nullification we're not talking about the crime committed by the accused but the actions of the government in bringing the subject to trial, and other moral dilemmas.

Excessive force/police cruelty to elicit a confession.

Excessively long interrogation and/or not providing proper food and water. Especially of a young person.

Cruel Incarceration. Seven months in solitary confinement for 23 hours a day prior to trial.

Convincing a mildly retarded person to commit a crime, he believing he's helping the police, then arrested and prosecuted.

Religious beliefs. Religious organization employees subject to arrest for not following a law or regulation which is against their belief.

In a nutshell, it would be any willful and wanton conduct against due process and fundamental fairness that would shock your conscience.

Definition of Conscience. (Shortened version).

The moral sense: the faculty of judging the moral qualities of actions, or of discriminating between right and wrong; particularly applied to one's perception and judgment of the moral qualities of his own conduct, ...

"You don't have to leave your conscience at the courthouse door."

If you vote your conscience you'll never lose a night's sleep over your decision.

Conclusion

"You have the power but do you have the moral right?"

You cannot just make your vote based on nothing or a pet peeve. In the preceding entries you learned many reasons why you should vote Not Guilty, e.g., nullify the jury. But let's analyze some examples.

During slavery, Abolitionist would help run-away slaves which was against the law. Northern juries would not convict as they felt that slavery was immoral and evil. They had the power, and they believed they also had the moral right.

For years juries in the South would not convict a white man charged with assaulting a black man. Again they had the power, but did they have the moral right.

When none of the standards are present for nullification then your vote most probably should be "Guilty.

The Criminal Justice system doesn't like hung juries. It causes dropping the charges or a new trial, which is costly. When a jury cannot reach a verdict, the judge will usually call the jury back into the courtroom, and read it the "Chip Smith Charge." (Chip Smith is the name of a CT case).

Which in a nutshell says that you might consider the opinions of the others who have equal intelligence and heard the same evidence. But the opinion must be yours and yours alone.

You should listen to the charge by the judge and seriously consider it. If you feel the same, after careful deliberation, then your vote should still be "Not Guilty."

Author's Note: I hope and pray that all good citizens will stop trying to avoid jury duty. Then, and only then will we be able to preserve our freedoms by nullifying unconstitutional and unjust laws and regulations.

I hope you've enjoyed this chapter as much as I have in writing it.

APPENDIX A

Words & Acronyms
& Initialisms

Some people have called me a wordsmith.

I don't believe that I am.
But when I see a word that I like,
I look up the definition and put it in my
Word List.

If you google only one word out of everyone
of your blogs before posting,
You'll be a wordsmith in one year.
As so many won't ever do it . . . it must
be blissful to remain ignorant.

In No Special Order

Acronym - a word formed from the initial letter or letters of each of the successive parts or major parts of a compound term. NASA – National Aeronautical & Space Agency.

Initialism - an abbreviation formed from initial letters. FBI – Federal Bureau of Investigation.

What is the difference?

An acronym is when the letters can be sounded as a word where an initialism, the letters cannot be sounded like a word. Some people say that initialisms are also acronyms.

IDK – is an initialism as it cannot be sounded out as a word. I don't know what this one means as I've asked all my friends and they've all told me, "I Don't Know." I guess no one does.

Metaphor – a figure of speech in which a word or phrase literally denoting one kind of object or idea is used in place of another to suggest a likeness. He's a bear when he wakes up in the morning. A=A.

Simile - a figure of speech comparing two unlike things that is often introduced by *like* or *as*. He's like a bear when he wakes up in the morning. A=B. Metaphor, is a bear; Simile, like a bear.

Paradox – a statement that is seemingly contradictory . . . and yet is perhaps true.

The book title, *Empty When Half Full*, by Patrick Forsyth is a wonderful example.

"Less is More." Using white space. White space, also known as negative space, is the open space between the design elements on your site. This empty area amid text, images, logos, and so on helps guide users' eyes from place to place, telling them where to focus their attention. Though white space is often overlooked, it is an important aspect of effective Web design. *Design it Yourself,* by Avi Itzkowitch and Adam Till. (Pg. 152).

Collywobbles – intestinal disturbance, belly ache. (I just like how it sounds).

Pejorative – a word expressing contempt or disapproval.

Double entendre - a word or expression capable of two interpretations with one usually risque.

Formication –

1. an abnormal sensation similar to that of insects crawling over or under the skin.
2. Uncontrollable itching. The more you scratch the worse it gets.

Bumfuzzle – confused, perplexed, fluster.

Obturation – the swelling of a cartridge after firing making it difficult to remove spent cartridges.

Quale – a property considered apart from things having the property. The bright red color of the car seemed to jump out at you. It appears to be a quality of its own, but the paint belongs to the car.

Dittohead – one who mindlessly agrees with an idea or opinion. (Don't be a dittohead. Do your own thinking).

Non Sequitur – a statement that is not connected in a logical or clear way to anything said before it. "We were talking about the new restaurant when she threw in some *non sequitur* about her dog."

Eristic – of or characterized by debate or argument. Aiming at winning rather than at reaching the truth.

Tautology – the same thing is said twice in different words. "Let's all work together, everyone." Or, "Let's work together."

Brabble – To argue over petty matters.

Entropy – gradual decline into disorder.

Craven – having or showing a complete lack of courage: very cowardly.

Misogynist – a person who dislikes, . . . or is strongly prejudiced against women.

Homonym - one of two or more words spelled and pronounced alike but different in meaning – bear, a wild animal and bear, to put up with.

1. Homophones, which are homonyms, are spelled differently, but sound the same.
2. Homographs are also homonyms, are spelled the same and sound the same, but have different meanings.

If one wants to find my other favorite words, he merely has to look in a dictionary,

There are 500,000 words in the English language.

Write Your Favorite Words Here

1._____

_____

2._____

_____

3._____

_____

4._____

_____

5._____

_____

APPENDIX B

Quotations & Ponderables

People with a personal agenda should not be
In charge of anything,
Except their own personal agenda.

Quotations

"It's never wrong to do the right thing." – Dr. Rick Rigsby.

From his speech given at the Maritime Academy. His book, *Lessons From A Third Grade Dropout.*

"No one has to be tolerant of evil." – Anon.

"A subject is told what to do by his government. A citizen tells his government what to do." – Anon.

"We the people are the rightful masters of both Congress and the courts, not to overthrow the Constitution but to overthrow the men who pervert the Constitution." – Abraham Lincoln.

"The intuitive mind is a sacred gift, and the rational mind is a faithful servant. We have created a society that honors the servant and has forgotten the gift." – Albert Einstein.

"An armed man is a citizen. A disarmed man is a subject." – Allen West.

"Stupid is like being dead. In both cases, you don't know you are." – Anon.

"A smart man only believes half of what he hears, a wise man knows which half."

- Col. Jeff Cooper.

"The only exercise that some people get is jumping to conclusions." – Gm York.

"Man can only take away your life. God can take away your eternity." – Anon.

My Ponderables & Thoughts

I never could find the definition of police officer in a dictionary—only in my conscience.

Politically correct speech = Lying.

There is no such place as a Gun-Free Zone.

The word regulated, in a well regulated militia, means well trained, not well controlled.

It is not a lie to answer any way you want to a question that is improper, immoral, one that may violate your rights or privacy, or whether the answer may do harm to an innocent.

If you have to do stupid things to prove to yourself that you are a man . . . you're not!

Life is simple; stupidity makes it complicated.

There are no leaders. They are merely a reflection of the people who voted for them. While one is criticizing his leaders, one should be looking in a mirror.

Stop calling our elected officials names, call those who elected them names.

People who don't vote, do not have the right to complain about the results.

If you believe that you may not like the answer to your question; don't ask it.

Answers are based on the belief of the one questioned, not on the belief of the questioner.

You stop maturing at the age where you are stopped being nurtured.

Ignorance is bliss . . . to your enemies.

Phases of Cognizance

Cognizance - knowledge, awareness.

I think - One's own feelings. Usually when one starts a comment with the words, "I think." It usually means that he didn't.

I believe - Perception of what one believes to be true.

I know - Knowledge based on facts known, prior experience, training, and education.

None of the above is proof that the information put forth is correct, but merely indicates the author's depth of thought.

Education, 19th Century v. Today

Recently I read a letter that was posted in Boston, Mass., on Feb. 15th, 1855. Who wrote this letter written in almost perfect English, as to structure, punctuation, etc.? It was written by a runaway slave. Although some slaves, without any schooling, taught themselves to read and write it was against the law. If caught they would suffer severe punishment.

Last year I read another letter. That one had perfect spelling, sentence structure and punctuation. It was written, in cursive writing, in1880 by a wild young man who was killed at age 24. This young man probably never got past the 5th grade. His name was Billy the Kid.

One written by a runaway slave in 1855 and the other by a young outlaw in 1880 and both are superior to most writings of today.

Truth

"The minute someone demonstrates courage and tells the truth, she has moved within the spheres of influence to a point where her inner world changes and the person begins to have an increase of her personal power and integrity. While the negative feelings have not all disappeared, the person has greater energy to handle nasty situations. She is no longer living in the world of victimhood. When someone will not acknowledge or tell the truth, she lives within her own creation of lack and limitation. Without truth, unconditional love is not possible, as people are ruled by their own selfishness, in which other people are merely objects to satisfy their needs and wants." Quoted from the book, *When All Hell Breaks Loose,* by Cody Lundin. (An excellent book on survival).

Politically correct speech, on the other hand, is one where the facts have to be changed to satisfy the speaker's personal agenda; therefore, it is a lie. Only the truth, (actual facts), the whole truth, (not leaving facts out), and nothing but the truth, (not adding information that would tend to enhance the speaker's personal point), is required for it to be the truth and not a lie.

Pity the poor person, a coward, always afraid that someone may not like him, who always must utter politically correct speech, instead of what he wants to say, or what he feels should be said . . . but, alas, cannot. Only the truth can calm the heart.

Phases of Surrender

Jeff Cooper summed it up when he wrote: "Fight back! Whenever you are offered violence, fight back! The aggressor does not fear the law, so he must be taught to fear you. Whatever the risk, and at whatever the cost, fight back!" Which says it all, but the following goes into more detail.

The Phases of Surrender

The first phase of surrender is failing to be armed, trained and committed to fight. We are prepared to surrender when we are unprepared to resist.

The second phase of surrender is failing to be alert. You must see trouble coming in order to have time to respond. The warning may be less than one second but it will be there and it must be recognized and acted upon immediately.

The Third phase of surrender is giving up your weapons.

The last phase of surrender is up to the monsters who have taken control of your life and perhaps the lives of your loved ones. The last phase of surrender is out of your hands.

Surrender during war

During the American Revolution 12,000 Colonists captured by the British died in captivity on prison ships, while only 8,000 died in battle. Had the 12,000 who surrendered continued to fight many would have survived and they could have done great damage to the British and likely shortened the war.

Civil War prisoners were treated so badly that some 50,000 died in captivity. More Americans have been killed by Americans than by any foreign army in any war. Six hundred eighteen thousand (618,000) Americans died in the Civil War.

As many as 18,000 captured American and Filipino prisoners died or were murdered at the hands of the Japanese during the six days of the "Bataan Death March." Had most of these soldiers slipped into the jungle and fought as guerrillas they could have tied up elements of the Japanese Army for months or years and perhaps more of them would have survived the war. Of the Americans who actually reached Japanese prison camps during the war, nearly 50,000 died in captivity. That is more than 10 percent of all the American military deaths in the entire war in both the Pacific and European theaters combined. In addition to the 50,000 captured Americans who died in Japanese prison camps an additional 20,000 were murdered before reaching a prison camp. If those 70,000 Americans had continued to fight, they could have provided time for the United States to build and maneuver its forces, perhaps shortening the war and saving even more lives. Some of them would have likely survived the war. If they had all died in battle their fate would have been no worse.

During the early stages of the Battle of the Bulge American soldiers were massacred by the German troops who captured them.

During the Vietnam conflict many American Prisoners Of War were tortured daily for years by the Communist North Vietnamese. Many

Americans died during the process. Only Officers (Aviators) held in North Vietnam were ever repatriated. Enlisted Americans captured in South Viet Nam were routinely tortured, mutilated and murdered by the Communists.

As a combat soldier and knowing my fate should I be captured, I was committed to fighting to the death. I made specific plans to force the enemy to kill me rather than allow myself to be captured.

In recent years, American troops captured by Islamic terrorists groups have virtually all been tortured and murdered in gruesome fashion. If I were fighting in the Middle East, I would make a similar vow and plan to fight to the death. Under no circumstances would I allow myself to be captured by our Islamic enemies.

Death by Government

R.J. Rummel, who wrote the book, "Death by Government" states that prior to the 20th Century; 170 million civilians were murdered by their own governments. Historians tell us that during the 20th Century perhaps as many as 200 million civilians were murdered by their own governments.

Some of the Nations where the mass murder of civilians occurred during the 20th Century include Russia, Ukraine, Germany, Poland, Czechoslovakia, The Congo, Uganda, Armenia, Viet Nam, Cambodia, Nigeria, Laos, China, Cuba, Manchuria, Iraq, Iran, Biafra, Rwanda and many others. The slaughter of civilians by governments appears to be as common as not.

Most of these slaughters were only made possible by disarming the victims before killing them. Had these people resisted, their fate would have been no worse and perhaps better. Resistance is much more difficult after the government has already taken the means of resistance away from the people. Planned genocide has been the primary reason for weapon confiscation throughout history.

Jews and others who surrendered to the Nazis were murdered in slave labor camps by the millions. Had all the Jews in Europe resisted when the Nazis started rounding them up they could have made the Nazis pay an enormous price for the holocaust. The fact that Hitler confiscated guns in 1936 made resistance far less feasible.

Had the Jews in Germany resisted, the outcome may have been the same but the world would have learned about the holocaust years earlier and may have intervened. Most people would prefer to die fighting and trying to kill their oppressor, than be taken off to a death camp and starved to death or murdered in a gas chamber.

William Ayers, former leader of the Terrorist organization The Weather Underground, and close friend of Barack Obama, told his followers in the Weather Underground, When we (Communist Revolutionaries) take over the United States, we will have to kill 25 million Americans. He was referring to those who would never submit to a Communist takeover. Those who would refuse to deny and reject the Constitution would have to be murdered. If this sounds impossible, remember that Genocide by Government was the leading cause of death in the last Century.

Surrendering to Criminals

The Onion Field Murder in California was a wake up call to Law Enforcement Officers everywhere. On March 9, 1963, two Los Angeles Police Department officers were taken prisoner by two criminals. The Officers submitted to capture and gave up their weapons.

They were driven to an onion field outside of Bakersfield.

One Officer was murdered while the other Officer managed to escape in a hail of gunfire. The surviving Officer suffered serious psychological distress, having been unable to save his partner. As a result of this incident, the LAPD policy became, You will fight no matter how bad things are. You will never ever surrender your weapons or yourself to a criminal.

Consider the Ogden, Utah record store murders. Read the book if you do not know the story. The manner in which the criminals murdered their young victims cannot be described here. Resistance might have been futile. Compliance was definitely and absolutely futile.

The courts in this country have ruled that the police have no legal obligation to protect anyone. Why do Law Enforcement Officials always tell civilians not to resist a criminal, while they tell their Officers to always resist and never surrender? Police administrators fear being sued by a civilian victim who gets hurt resisting. Furthermore, the police, like all government agencies derive their power by fostering dependence.

According to Professor John Lott's study on the relationship between guns and crime, a victim who resists with a firearm is less likely to be hurt or killed than a victim who cooperates with his attacker. His book is titled "More Guns, Less Crime."

The Doctor and his family in Connecticut complied and cooperated, meeting every demand of the home invasion robbers to whom they had surrendered. The Doctor's wife and daughters were tortured, raped, doused with gasoline and burned alive. How did surrender and cooperation work out for them?

In another home invasion robbery, a kindly couple with 9 adopted, special needs children, surrendered to the robbers. The victims opened their safe and did not resist in any way. When the robbers where finished ransacking the home and terrifying the children, they shot both parents in the head several times before leaving. How did surrender and complete cooperation work out for them?

Handing over your life by surrendering to someone who is in the process of committing a violent crime against you is a form of suicide. Some survive but many do not. The monster gets to decide for you. We have heard brutalized victims say, "The robber said that he would not hurt us if we cooperated." Why would you believe anything that someone who is committing a crime against you says? He will be lying if he speaks. As we say in law enforcement, If a criminal's lips are moving while he is speaking, he is lying. Criminals by definition are dishonest and should never be trusted or believed. You have no doubt heard friends say, I would not resist a criminal, after all why would he kill me? This is stupid and naive. In law enforcement, we call these people "Victims by Choice" (VBC). There could be a long list of reasons why a criminal would kill you despite your cooperation.

You may be of a different race, thus a different tribe. Only members of his tribe are actually human in his mind. He may feel hatred toward you because you have more than he does. Gratification from being in a position of total power is reason enough for some.

Criminals are sometimes members of a Satanic Cult who worship death such as the "Night Stalker" in California. Eliminating a potential witness is often cited as a reason to kill a victim. Sometimes criminals simply enjoy causing suffering and death. There are people who are in fact, pure evil. I have heard criminals say, "I killed her just to watch her die."

A victim who begs for mercy can give his attacker a tremendous feeling of power which many criminals seem to enjoy. You cannot expect mercy from someone who does not know what mercy is.

Resist! We each have a duty to ourselves, our loved ones, our neighbors, our community, our city, our state and our country to resist criminals. Reasoning with a thug who believes that his failures are because of people just like you is not likely to be helpful. Pleading with a terrorist who has been taught from birth that his salvation depends on murdering people like you is a doomed plan. Resist!

Resist! His gun may not be real. After you are tied up it will not matter. His gun may not be loaded. After you are tied up it will not matter. He may not know how to operate his gun. After you are tied up it will not matter.

Resist! Statistically if you run and your assailant shoots at you he will miss. Statistically if you run and he shoots and hits you, you will not die. Bad guys shooting at the police miss 90 percent of the time. The odds are on your side. Better to die fighting in place than to be tied up, doused with gasoline and burned alive. There are things worse than death. Surrender to a criminal or a terrorist and you will learn what they are.

Resist! If you resist with a commitment to win you may well prevail, especially if you are armed and trained. If you lose it is still better to die fighting in place than to be taken prisoner and have your head cut off with a dull knife while your screams gurgle through your own blood as we have witnessed on numerous videos from the Middle East, brought to us by the "Islamic practitioners of peace."

Some who have refused to surrender

History is filled with brave people who refused to surrender. Some of these men and woman have won their battles despite what seemed to be insurmountable odds. Others have gone down fighting and avoided being tortured to death. Some fought to the death to help or save others. Many have fought to the death for an idea or a belief.

When General Santa Ana (also the President of Mexico at the time) ordered 180 "Texacans" to surrender the Alamo, Col. Travis answered with "a cannon shot and a rebel yell." Eventually General Santa Ana was able to build his troop strength to ten thousand. The Mexicans then swarmed the defenders and killed them all. The battle of the Alamo delayed the Mexican Army long enough for Sam Houston to build his Texacan Army, which met and defeated the Mexican Army and captured General Santa Ana. General Santa Ana traded Texas for his life and the sacrifices of the Alamo defenders changed history.

Frank Luke was a heroic aviator in WWI. Shot down and wounded he refused to surrender when confronted by a German patrol. He killed 4 German soldiers with his 1911 Pistol before being killed. Luke was posthumously awarded the Medal of Honor.

When his unit was pinned down by German Machine Guns and all of the Officers and non-commissioned officers in his company were killed or wounded, Alvin York never considered surrendering. Instead, he attacked hundreds of German soldiers killing about 25 with his rifle and pistol and then captured 132 others by himself!

Most of the Jews in the Warsaw Ghetto (Poland) surrendered to the German Army. They were taken off to death camps and murdered. Between 400 and 1,000 Jews refused to surrender and armed with only a few pistols, revolvers and rifles, they held off the German Army for three months before dying in battle.

During the "Battle of the Bulge," the 101st Airborne was surrounded by the German Army and ordered to surrender. Faced with overwhelming odds, the Commanding Officer of the 101st sent this reply to the Germans. "Nuts." The Americans refused to surrender and they stopped the German advance. Most of the American troops survived.

On Sept 2, 2010, 40 armed criminals took over and robbed a train in India. Some of the robbers had guns, others used knives and clubs. When they began to disrobe an 18 year old girl for the purpose of gang raping her, one of the passengers decided to fight. He was a 35 year old retired Gurkha soldier. He drew his Khukasri knife and attacked the 40 robbers. He killed three of the robbers and wounded 8 more despite his being wounded in this 20 minute fight. The remaining criminals fled for their lives leaving their stolen loot and eleven comrades dead or wounded on the floor of the train. The eight wounded robbers were arrested. How does one man defeat 40?

How does he summon the courage to fight such odds? He utilized all of the Principles of Personal Defense: Alertness, Decisiveness, Aggressiveness, Speed, Coolness, Ruthlessness, and Surprise. He was skilled in the use of his weapon. Most importantly, He refused to be a victim and allow evil to triumph! If this one inspirational soldier can defeat 40 opponents using his knife, it would seem that we should all be able to defeat a group of armed criminals by using our firearms if we are professionally trained as was this heroic Gurkha soldier.

Final thoughts

How will you respond if you are confronted by evil as some of us have been in the past and some of us will be in the future? If you have not decided ahead of time what you will do, you will likely do nothing. Those who fight back often win and survive. Those who surrender never win and often die a horrible death. Have you made your decision? Remember, no decision is a decision to do nothing.

The "principles" named in the retired Ghurka in the story near the end come from Jeff Cooper's "Principles of Personal Defense," which is a must-read in my opinion. It is only 45 pages including illustrations and blank pages between chapters. When someone asks me for advice in buying a gun for defense, I loan them a copy of this book. If they read it and still want help, I am willing to do all I can. If they refuse it or return it unread, and cannot take the time to read a 45-page book on this serious matter, they are on their own because they have shown me they do not grasp the situation. Or don't want to.

I try to read it once a year to keep my mind right, It is about that time again.—Anon.

Notes

Notes

About the Author

After serving in the U.S. Navy during the Korean War and the China Campaign, Nate attended several schools and held a number of jobs in industry. In 1970 he started his Law Enforcement career and earned the honor of "Top Gun" during his academy class.

After making Lieutenant, Nate spent 19 years as a full-time instructor at the Connecticut Police Academy. During this time he was a guest lecturer on several subjects and at many venues, such as the Smith & Wesson Academy, was appointed Director of police training for Northeastern Connecticut by the Connecticut Criminal Justice Planning and Supervisory Board, and an Invitee under the President's Ambassador Program to teach police firearm instructors in Russia and China.. Especially fulfilling was lecturing on Child Abuse for 11 years to first responders, teachers, and medical personnel.

After he retired, he moved to Denver, CO where he spent several years as a Private Eye and taught at a local college.

As an author of several books and an expert in firearms and criminal law, Nate currently follows his passion for educating others through online media.

He has been recognized for his achievements in:

Who's Who in American Law Enforcement,
Who's Who in the East,
Who's Who in America.
Who's Who in the World.

Printed in the United States
By Bookmasters